REALLY, RAPUNZEL NEEDED A HAIRCUT!

The Story of
RAPUNZEL
as Told by
DAME GOTHEL

by
Jessica Gunderson

illustrated by
Denis Alonso

PICTURE WINDOW BOOKS
a capstone imprint

Special thanks to our adviser, Terry Flaherty, PhD, Professor of English,
Minnesota State University, Mankato, for his expertise.

⋅◦⚜⋅⚜⋅⚜◦⋅

Editor: Jill Kalz
Designer: Lori Bye
Art Director: Nathan Gassman
Production Specialist: Jennifer Walker
The illustrations in this book were created digitally.

⋅◦⚜⋅⚜⋅⚜◦⋅

Picture Window Books
1710 Roe Crest Drive
North Mankato, MN 56003
www.capstonepub.com

Library of Congress Cataloging-in-Publication Data
Cataloging-in-publication information is on file with the Library of Congress.
ISBN 978-1-4048-7941-6 (library binding)
ISBN 978-1-4795-1946-0 (paper over board)
ISBN 978-1-4795-1950-7 (paperback)
ISBN 978-1-4795-1884-5 (eBook PDF)

Printed in the United States of America
in Stevens Point, Wisconsin.
032013   007227WZF13

Let me tell you, it's lonely being a witch. When folks find out what I am, they steer clear. I have no friends at all. Not one. It's unfair, really.

A sweet girl with beautiful hair once lived with me. And I used to have a fantastic garden. (Neither the girl nor the plants cared one whit that I was a witch.) My flowers bloomed bright and tall. My radishes were to die for. But, sadly, I haven't seen the girl or my garden in a while. It all started when a neighbor tried to *steal* my radishes ...

Here's how it went:

"My wife is going to have a baby," my neighbor stammered. "And she craves your radishes. She swears if she doesn't get them, she'll just die!"

4

"OK," I said. "But what will you give me in return? I can get a pretty penny for these at the Farmers' Market, you know."

"But I have no money. Not a single dime!" he whined. "Maybe I'll give you our baby? We can always have more, I guess."

Of course I agreed. A baby would be better than gold! It would cure my loneliness!

When the time came, the man brought baby Rapunzel to me. I raised Rapunzel as my own daughter and gave her anything she wanted from my garden: turnips, potatoes, berries, cucumbers ... But do you know what her favorite food was?

Radishes.

The girl had good taste.

All those vegetables helped Rapunzel's hair grow long and red. She sang sweet songs as she helped me tend the garden.

The longer Rapunzel's hair grew, the more she loved it. She washed it and combed it and brushed it and braided it. And then she washed it again. You have no idea how much I spent on shampoo.

One day a group of neighbors gathered outside my garden. I heard them whispering. Plotting. Planning. This time, however, no one wanted to steal my radishes. Nope. They wanted to steal *Rapunzel* and use her hair for wigs!

Radish

So I did what any mother would do.
I locked the girl away in a tower.

10

"Rapunzel, let down your hair!"

I would call. And she would lean out of the window and wrap her hair around a hook. Then I'd climb up.

Every day without fail, I brought her vegetables from the garden. At first she seemed content. But one day she told me she was lonely. And if anyone knows how loneliness feels, it's me. "How can I help?" I asked.

"Bring me every mirror you can find," Rapunzel said.

"Then I can keep myself company."

13

Hauling a load of mirrors to the tower wasn't my idea of fun, but I did it anyway. I spent a week gathering every mirror in the village. Then I lugged them, one by one, into the tower. Let me tell you, it was not an easy task for an old witch like me.

"Thanks!" Rapunzel said. "But I don't need the mirrors anymore. I met a handsome prince. He climbs up to visit me every day."

"What?" I roared, my voice rattling the windows and shattering the mirrors.

"He's going to steal you away!"

I panicked. What could I do? How could I keep the prince away? In a blink I grabbed Rapunzel's hair and chopped it off. Clumps of it.

16

Rapunzel wailed. I admit I felt a little bad. "It'll grow back," I comforted.

"Short hair will be nice for the summer. Cooler."

But she would not stop crying.

"Let's go home, dear," I said. "I'll make you a radish salad, OK?" I fastened her hair clippings to the hook, and we crawled down together.

While Rapunzel chomped her salad, I returned to the tower and waited.

"Rapunzel! Let down your hair!" the prince called.

I lowered Rapunzel's hair, and the prince climbed up.

19

When the prince saw me, his eyes widened. I gave him my most evil cackle.

I'd meant only to scare him a little, but he leaped out of the window and landed on some thorny bushes below. The poor boy staggered about, clutching his eyes. I was going to climb down and help him, but he did a terrible thing. He reached for Rapunzel's hair and yanked it from the hook. Then he ran away.

Since then I've been trapped in this tower. I try to sing sweetly in hopes of rescue, but my voice is sour. I try to grow my hair long, but my split-ends keep breaking off. Drat those mirrors for bringing me bad luck!

A little bird told me Rapunzel and her prince got married. I'm sorry I missed the wedding. It sounded lovely. Do you know what the bride carried? A bouquet of radish roses!

Critical Thinking Using the Common Core

Look online to find the original story. Describe how the character of the witch, Dame Gothel, looks and acts. Compare and contrast that witch with the witch in this version of the story. (Integration of Knowledge and Ideas)

If Rapunzel told the story instead of Dame Gothel, what details might she tell differently? What if the prince told the story? How would his point of view differ? (Craft and Structure)

Dame Gothel never says she loves Rapunzel in this story, but she does. How do we know this? How does Dame Gothel show Rapunzel that she loves her? What does Dame Gothel say that tells us she cares about this girl? (Key Ideas and Details)

Glossary

character—a person, animal, or creature in a story
point of view—a way of looking at something
version—an account of something from a certain point of view

Read More

Bradman, Tony. *Rapunzel Lets Her Hair Down.* After Happily Ever After. Mankato, Minn.: Stone Arch Books, 2009.

Peters, Stephanie True, retold by. *Rapunzel: The Graphic Novel.* Graphic Spin. Minneapolis, Minn.: Stone Arch Books, 2009.

Zelinsky, Paul O., retold and illustrated by. *Rapunzel.* New York: Dutton Children's Books, 1997.

Internet Sites

FactHound offers a safe, fun way to find Internet sites related to this book. All of the sites on FactHound have been researched by our staff.

Here's all you do:
Visit *www.facthound.com*
Type in this code: 9781404879416

Look for all the books in the series:

Believe Me, Goldilocks Rocks!
Frankly, I Never Wanted to Kiss Anybody!
Honestly, Red Riding Hood Was Rotten!
No Kidding, Mermaids Are a Joke!
No Lie, I Acted Like a Beast!

Really, Rapunzel Needed a Haircut!
Seriously, Cinderella Is SO Annoying!
Seriously, Snow White Was SO Forgetful!
Truly, We Both Loved Beauty Dearly!
Trust Me, Jack's Beanstalk Stinks!

Super-cool stuff! Check out projects, games and lots more at
www.capstonekids.com